Measure It with Math!

MEASURING DISTANCE

Anne O'Daly

PowerKiDS press

Published in 2024 by The Rosen Publishing Group, Inc.
2544 Clinton Street, Buffalo, NY 14224

Portions of this work were originally authored by Chris Woodford and published as *Distance*.
All new material this edition authored by Anne O'Daly.

Children's Publisher: Anne O'Daly

Design Manager: Keith Davis

Picture Manager: Sophie Mortimer

Picture credits:

Key: t = top, tr = top right, b = bottom

Front Cover: Shutterstock: flashpict tl, Prostock Sudio l, Tish1 tr, Georgios Tsichlis c;

Interior: Dreamstime: Robyn Mackenzie 12bc, Steve Mann 12br, Redazione745 22, Lawrence Welowski Jr 9t; iStock: Andrej67 25, exopixel 7, younggoldman 23; Shutterstock: Daily Travel Photos 6, gualtiro boffi 11b, Georghiou Christos 1, 28–29, Constantin Cornel 16, ekler 12b, Shaun Jeffers 10, Love Employee 17, maksimee 14, Cosmin Manei 11t, ONIONA 4, Tetiana Rostopira 12t, Pairoj Sroyngem 9b, atyana Tomsickova 18.

Cataloging-in-Publication Data

Names: O'Daly, Anne.
Title: Measuring distance / Anne O'Daly.
Description: New York : Powerkids Press, 2024. | Series: Measure it with math! | Includes glossary and index.
Identifiers: ISBN 9781642827767 (pbk.) | ISBN 9781642827774 (library bound) | ISBN 9781642827781 (ebook)
Subjects: LCSH: Distances--Measurement--Juvenile literature. | Weights and measures--Juvenile literature. | Measurement--Juvenile literature. | Mathematics--Juvenile literature.
Classification: LCC TA601.O34 2024 | DDC 530.8--dc23

Manufactured in the United States of America

CPSIA Compliance Information: Batch #CSPK24. For further information contact Rosen Publishing at 1-800-237-9932.

Contents

What Is Distance?

Distance tells us how long, tall, or far away something is. Length is a kind of distance. It measures from one end of an object to the other. Another kind of distance is height. This is how tall something is. The height of a building is the distance from the ground to the top.

The Empire State Building in New York City is 1,250 feet high.

DISTANCE = LENGTH

Distance and length are the same thing.
This line is 1 inch long

1 foot = 12 inches
1 yard = 3 feet = 36 inches
1 mile = 1,760 yards = 5,280 feet
= 63,360 inches

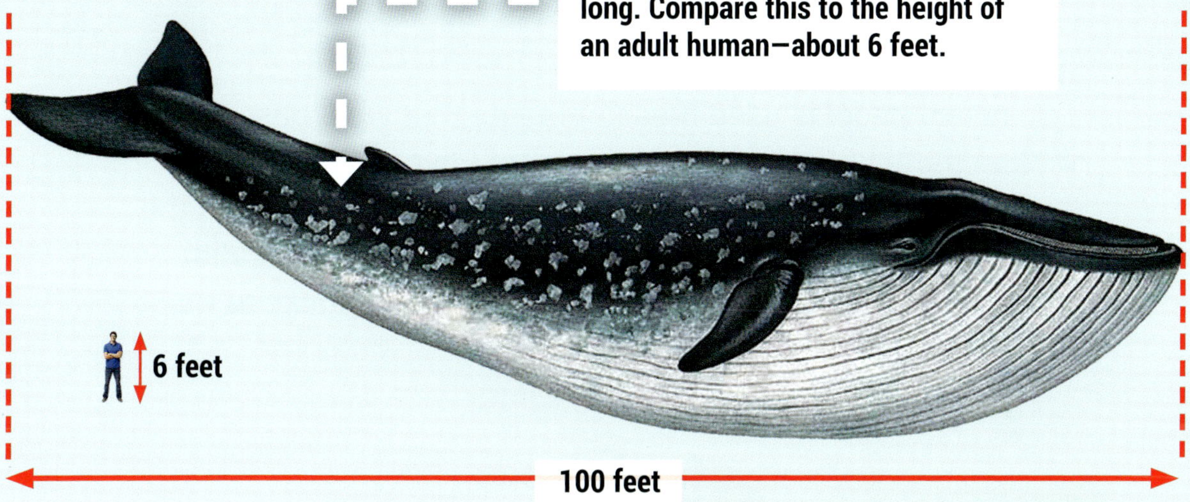

How to Measure Distance

We can measure distance along a straight line using different tools. They include wooden, plastic, or metal rulers. There are measuring tapes that bend. Laser beams (strong rays of light) measure distance. There are many ways of measuring distances on land, at sea, and even in space.

WHY DISTANCE MATTERS

There are lots of reasons why we need to measure distance. You might want to know if a pair of jeans will be long enough for your legs, or the right size for your waist. A person driving to another town needs to know how far away it is. That way, they can figure out how much gas to put in the tank and how long the journey will take.

Distance in Ancient times

Ancient peoples used measurements that were based on parts of their body. The ancient Egyptians invented a measurement called a cubit. This was the distance from the tip of the middle finger to the elbow. But the Egyptians did not use their arms to measure things. They cut sticks to the length of a cubit and used those.

The ancient Egyptians built huge structures such as these pyramids. They needed to measure distances accurately so that their buildings would stand up.

TRY THIS

HOW MANY FOREARMS?

Try measuring things using ancient methods. Ask an adult to stretch out his or her arm. Measure the arm from the middle finger to the elbow. That measurement is a cubit. Try measuring your bed, your sofa, or the length of a table in cubits.

Ancient Measurements

A: 1 cubit (the forearm)

B: 16 finger widths = 1 foot

C: 1 uncia = about 1 inch

D: 1 foot = about 12 inches

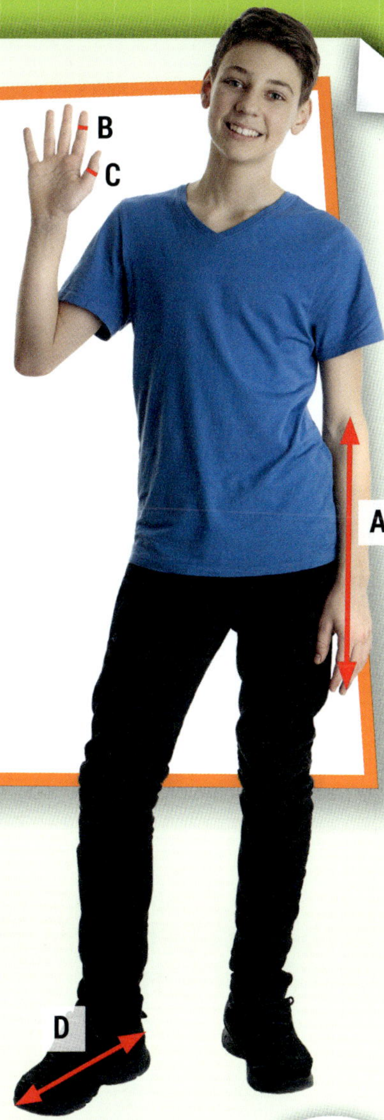

Fingers and Thumbs

Ancient Greeks lived about 2,500 years ago. They measured distance with the width of their fingers. Sixteen fingers was about the length of a person's foot. This is how the measurement "foot" got its name.

Ancient Romans had another way to measure. Instead of using fingers, they used the width of their thumb. They called this an uncia. The word "inch" comes from that name. The Romans found that a person's foot was usually about 12 inches long. We still have 12 inches in 1 foot.

Inches, Feet, and Yards

The ancient Romans measured an inch with their thumbs. About 1,000 years ago, people in England measured an inch by placing three ears of barley side by side. The distance across the barley was 1 inch. Using different measurements was confusing. If people selling cloth used different measures, no one knew how much cloth they were buying.

TRY THIS

CALCULATING DISTANCE

Below are distances using the imperial system.

The height of a typical adult person = 5 feet 9 inches.

How many inches is that?

The length of an average family car = 18 feet

How many inches is that?

The length of a football field = 120 yards

How many feet is that?

Answers on page 32.

The distance around Earth is 25,000 miles.

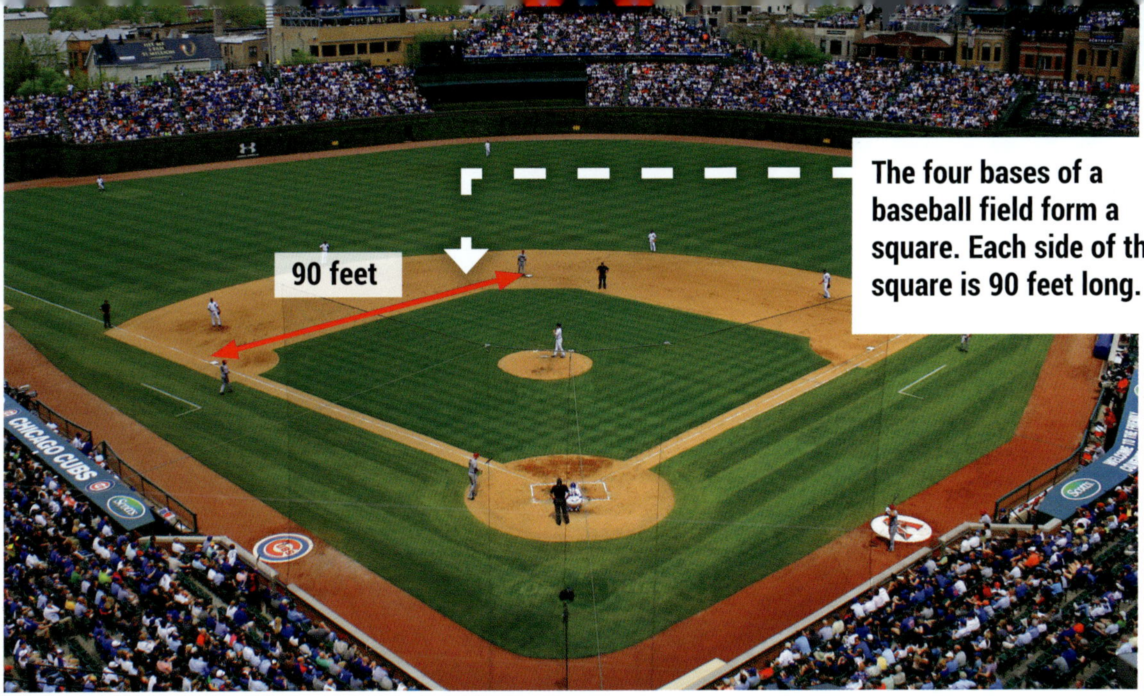

The four bases of a baseball field form a square. Each side of the square is 90 feet long.

Imperial System

The problem was solved in Europe several hundreds of years ago. This was during a time known as the Middle Ages. People began to use the same system of measurement. They had the inch, foot, yard, and mile. The system was called the imperial system. It is still used in many countries, including the United States.

People in England used to measure an inch by placing three ears of barley next to each other. It was not an accurate measure of distance.

Measure in Metric

The imperial system was better than the older systems, but many people found it hard to learn. Around 1800, some people in France came up with a different way to measure distances. It was much simpler. This was the metric system. It was based on a new length called the meter. One meter is 39 inches long, a little longer than a yard (3 feet, or 36 inches).

The metric system was first used in France in 1799. It was soon used all over Europe. The metric system is also called the International System, or SI system. It is used in most countries.

This signpost shows the distances to various cities in kilometers. New York is shown as being 15,008 kilometers away.

TRY THIS

MAKE IT METRIC

An adult flea is 3 millimeters long

This red line
is 1 centimeter long

1 centimeter = 10 millimeters

100 centimeters = 1 meter

1,000 meters = 1 kilometer

An elephant is 3 meters high.

* How tall are you (give your answer in meters and centimeters)?
* How long is your little finger (give your answer in centimeters and millimeters)?
* How tall is a page of this book (give your answer in centimeters and millimeters)?

Metric Units

The metric system is easier to remember than the imperial system. There are 10 millimeters (mm) in 1 centimeter (cm), 100 centimeters in 1 meter (m), and 1,000 meters in 1 kilometer (km). One centimeter is a little less than half an inch, and one kilometer is just over half a mile.

FACT

The original meter length, a bar made of platinum metal, is still kept in Paris, France.

Measuring Short Distances

A standard way to measure distance is to use a ruler. Rulers are pieces of wood, plastic, or metal. They are marked with measurements, such as inches or centimeters. Tape measures are bendy rulers. They have the same units of measurement as a ruler.

Long, flexible tape measures and rigid 12-inch rulers are tools that can be used to measure distance.

Rulers are usually 1 foot (30 centimeters) or 1 yard (90 centimeters). A one-yard ruler is called a yardstick. A one-meter ruler is a meterstick. It is 1 meter (39 inches) long.

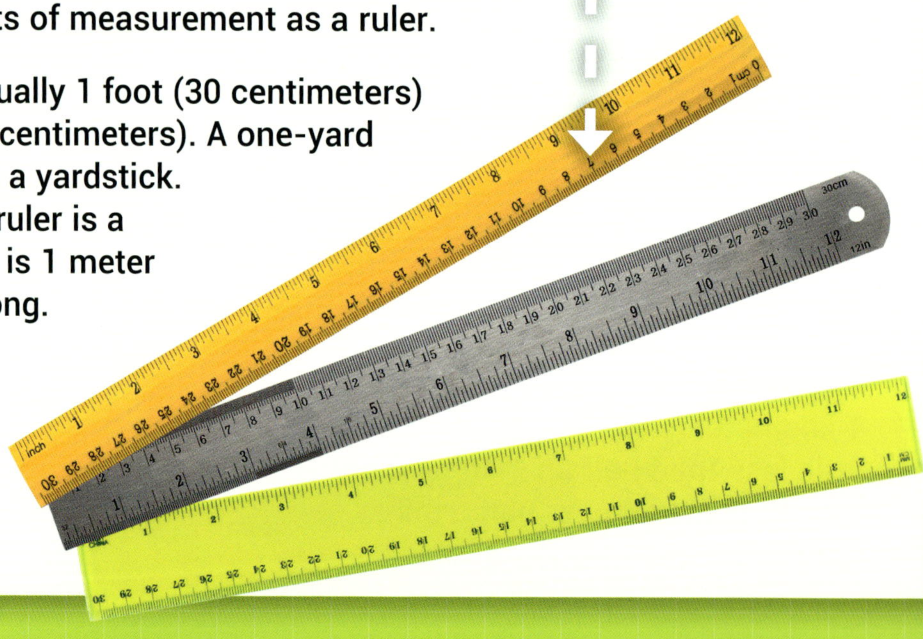

TRY THIS

CONVERTING IMPERIAL AND METRIC

We sometimes need to change imperial measurements into metric measurements, or metric into imperial measurements.

IMPERIAL TO METRIC

1 inch = 2.5 centimeters, or 25 millimeters

1 foot = 30 centimeters

1 yard = 90 centimeters

1 mile = 1,600 meters, or 1.6 kilometers

METRIC TO IMPERIAL

1 centimeter = 0.4 inch

1 meter = 3 feet 3 inches, or 39 inches

1 kilometer = 0.6 mile

* How many kilometers are there in 4 miles?
* How many centimeters are there in 4 inches?
* How many miles are there in 16 kilometers?

Longer Measurements

Rulers can also be used to measure distances that are longer than the ruler itself. Most rulers are marked with smaller units—inches, centimeters, or millimeters. We can measure longer things by moving the ruler along and counting how many times it fits into a distance.

This girl is 4 foot 6 inches, or 135 centimeters, tall.

Smaller Distances

Not all distances can be measured in a straight line. Sometimes people need to measure distances on a map or the thickness of small objects. They use special tools called dividers, calipers, or gauges.

Dividers are like the compasses we use to draw circles. To measure the distance between two points on a map, we open the two legs of the dividers. We put one leg on each point. Then the distance between the divider legs is measured against the map scale.

A digital caliper measures width and shows the measurement on a screen.

MICROMETER

A micrometer is a type of caliper with a built-in measuring scale. A micrometer is shaped like the letter C. It accurately measures the width of an object placed between its jaws.

This diagram shows how a micrometer could be used to measure the width of a steel marble.

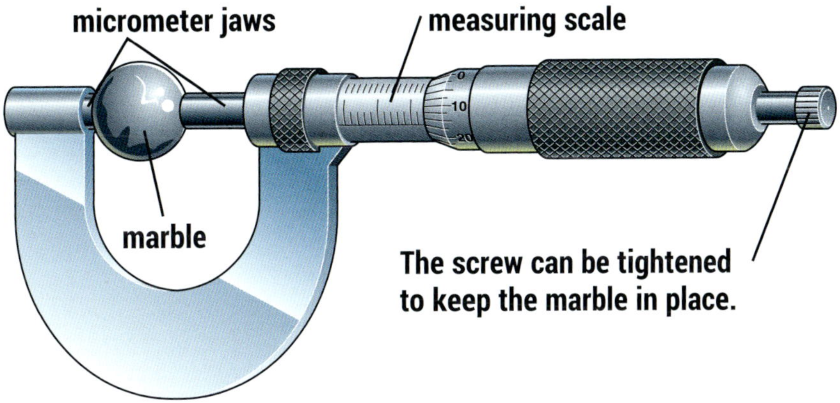

Calipers and Gauges

The width of an object can be measured by putting it in a caliper. When the object is removed, the distance between the caliper legs can be measured with a ruler, or the measurement shows on a digital screen.

A gauge has slots of different sizes cut into it. The width of a wire can be measured by matching it with the slot of the same size. The width can be read on the gauge.

FACT

The ancient Greeks used calipers. Some were found in a shipwreck dating back to the 6th century BCE.

Too Small to See

Some distances are too tiny to see with the naked eye. But we can still measure them. The size of a tiny bug can be measured with a microscope. This is a special tool that makes tiny objects look bigger. Some microscopes have a ruler built into the eyepiece. The size of the object can be measured by lining it up with this ruler.

This looks like a monster from a movie! But it's a beetle's head that has been magnified many times.

MEASURING TINY PARTICLES

Nanotechnology is an exciting area of science. It involves building new materials, medicines, and other things from incredibly tiny parts. Each part is just a few nanometers across. A nanometer (nm) is one-billionth of a meter. How small is that? A tiny speck of dust may be only about 3 nanometers wide. Put another way, if a nanometer were as wide as the head of a pin, a meter would be as far as the distance between Atlanta, Georgia, and Washington, D.C.!

Two tiny nanotubes made from minute particles called atoms.

Some microscope lenses magnify objects to about 10 times their normal size. Others can magnify things to about 1,500 times their normal size. These can measure body cells. They can even measure atoms. These are the tiny particles that make up everything in the universe.

FACT

Powerful microscopes can measure distances smaller than a speck of dust.

Measuring Long Distances

Rulers and microscopes are only useful for measuring small distances. Measuring long distances is more complicated. People planning the routes of new freeways, for example, need special tools.

Miles and miles of road stretch out across a desert. These long distances cannot be measured with rulers or tapes.

USING LASERS

People can measure long distances with laser beams! They use a machine called a theodolite. This sits on top of a tripod (a stand with three legs) to keep it steady. Another tripod, with a mirror on top, is placed at the point to be measured. The user presses a button, and the theodolite fires a laser beam toward the mirror. The beam bounces off the mirror back to the theodolite. A computer in the theodolite figures out the distance to the mirror. It shows the result on a screen. The answer is very accurate.

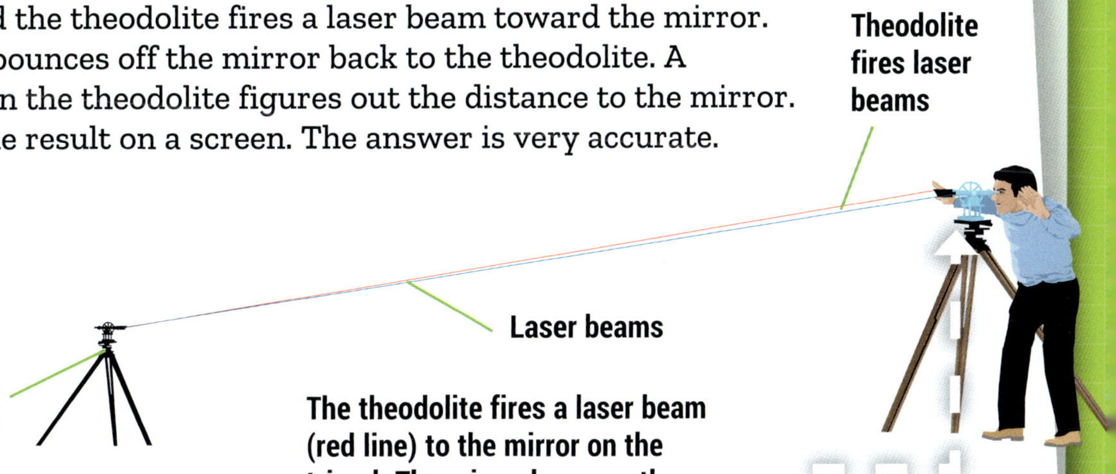

The theodolite fires a laser beam (red line) to the mirror on the tripod. The mirror bounces the beam back (blue line).

FACT

Light from a theodolite's laser travels at 186,000 miles per second (300,000 km/s).

Long Chains

In the past, people measured long distances using metal chains. Each chain had 100 metal links. Each link was 8 inches (20 cm) long, so the whole chain stretched to about 66 feet (20 meters). People measured distances by laying the chains end to end. It took 80 chains to measure 1 mile (1.6 kilometers).

Mapping Distances

How do we find out where we are going? We use a map! Maps show distances as well as places. They need to be accurate. A simple map is a picture of the countryside or a town seen from above. Maps can show cities, countries, and oceans. Many people use digital maps as well as paper maps.

TRY THIS

USING THE MAP

This is a map of the town shown on page 21.

* Can you work out where Main Street is on the map?
* Can you see where City Hall is on the map?
* Can you find the town's mall?

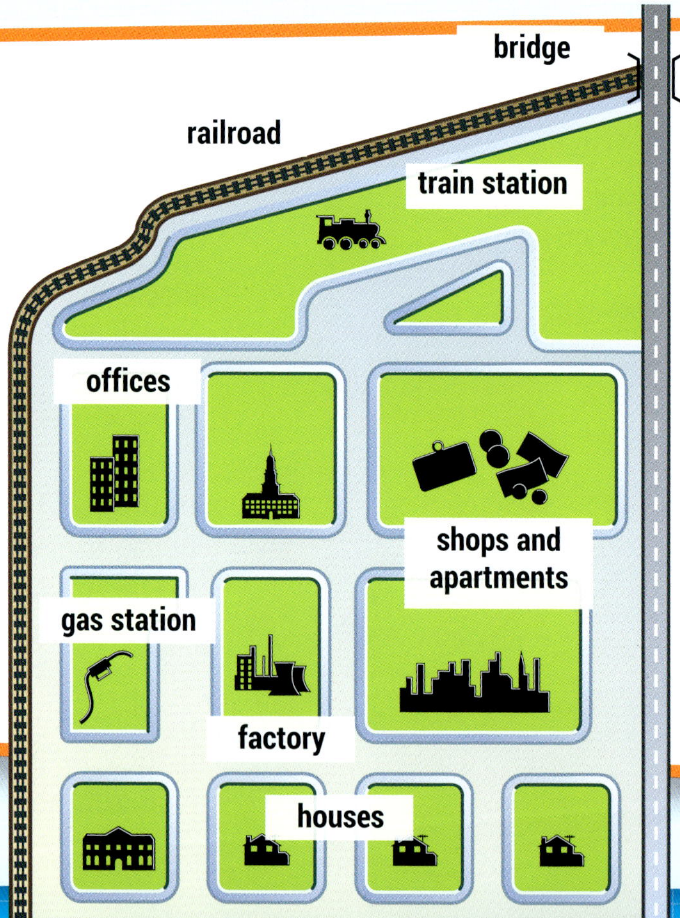

Map Scales

Maps usually have a scale (like a picture of a ruler) drawn on them. The scale shows how big the things on the map really are. The scale might show that 1 inch (2.5 cm) stands for 10 miles (16 km). So a street that is 1 inch (2.5 cm) long on the map is 10 miles (16 km) long in real life.

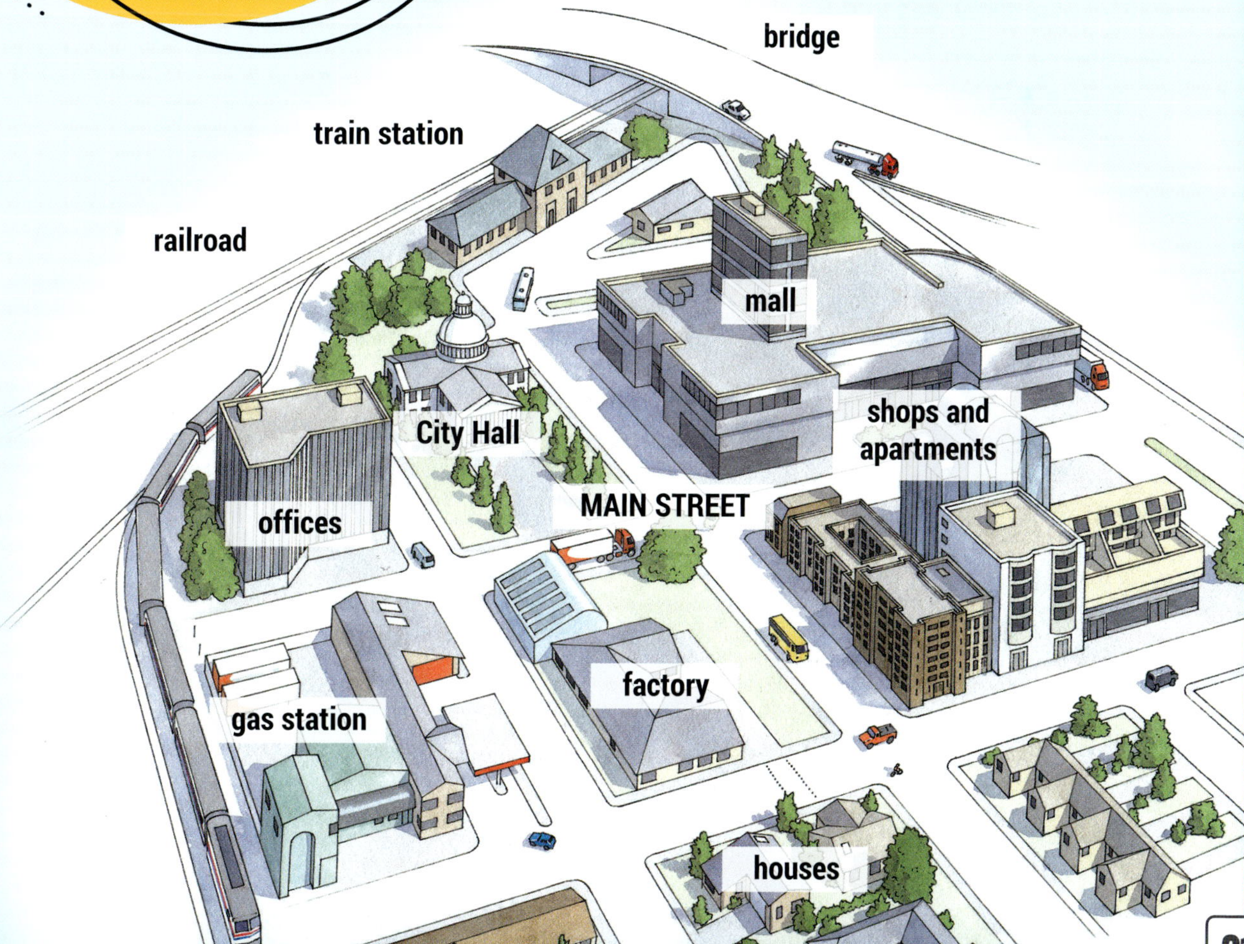

Travel and Distance

If people are traveling long distances, they might need to know how far they have gone. If they are traveling by car, an instrument on the dashboard measures the distance traveled. That instrument is called an odometer. It counts how many times the car's wheels turn around.

If a car wheel has a circumference of 60 inches (150 cm), the car has traveled 60 inches (150 cm) each time the wheel turns. An odometer counts how many times the wheel turns. Since it knows how big the wheel is, the odometer can figure out how far the car has traveled.

Italian cyclist Filippo Ganni won the world record in 2022 for cycling more than 35 miles (56.8 km) in one hour.

Pedometers

Walkers also use a device for measuring distance. It is called a pedometer. This jiggles as the person walks. It can work out how far the walker has traveled. Many people have pedometers in their smartphone or watch.

A hiker checks her watch to see how far she has walked. Some smartphones and watches show the number of steps and heart rate, as well as distance.

FACT

World record holder Andrew Andras skateboarded 261 miles (431 km) in just 24 hours!

ANIMAL TRAVELERS

Every year, some animals travel long distances from one place to another. These long trips are called migrations. Arctic terns make the longest journey of any animal. Each year, these birds fly from the Arctic to the Antarctic. Six months later, they fly back again. That's a round trip of nearly 50,000 miles (80,470 km)!

Measuring Distances at Sea

In the open sea, it can be hard to figure out where you are. They are no visual clues to help, like lighthouses or mountains. Navigation involves working out a position at sea or on land. Rough seas and bad weather can make it hard for ships to navigate.

SATELLITE NAVIGATION

Modern ships use satellites to navigate. This technology is called GPS, or Global Positioning System. A GPS receiver in a ship picks up signals from four different satellites. In a few seconds, the receiver can figure out a ship's position to within 50 feet (15 meters).

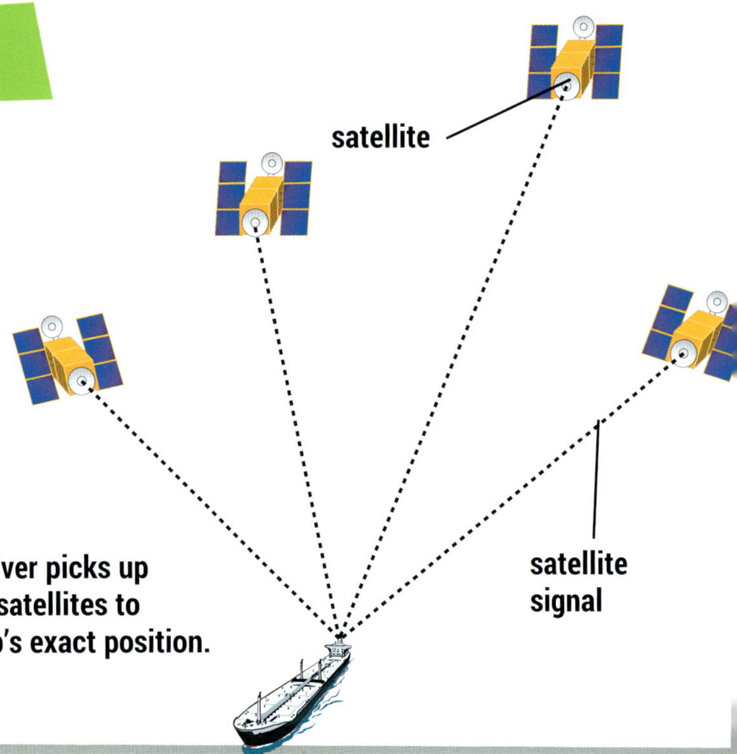

A ship's GPS receiver picks up signals from four satellites to figure out the ship's exact position.

FACT

Modern ships navigate using signals from satellites in space. This method is extremely accurate.

A sailor uses a sextant to measure how high the sun is in the sky. NEVER look at the sun. It can damage your eyes. A sextant has special shades.

The Sun and the Stars

Since ancient times, people have navigated by looking at the sun and the stars. Sailors used a tool called a sextant. It measured how high the sun is in the sky. This helped sailors figure out how far north or south the ship was.

If a ship moves at a steady speed in a straight line, sailors can also figure out how far the ship has sailed. This calculation is called dead reckoning.

Distances in Space

Space is huge! The tools we use on Earth cannot measure the enormous distances in space. Astronomers use powerful telescopes to see planets and stars. Some of these are on Earth. Others travel in space. The Hubble Space Telescope flies around Earth. It can see space objects that are millions of miles away.

OUR SOLAR SYSTEM

PLANET	DISTANCE FROM SUN
1. Mercury	37 million miles (60 million km)
2. Venus	65 million miles (105 million km)
3. Earth	93 million miles (150 million km)
4. Mars	130 million miles (209 million km)
5. Jupiter	484 million miles (778 million km)
6. Saturn	892 million miles (1,436 million km)
7. Uranus	1.78 billion miles (2.87 billion km)
8. Neptune	2.8 billion miles (4.5 billion km)
9. *Pluto	3.7 billion miles (5.9 billion km)

*dwarf planet

FACT

Scientists have only mapped 5 percent of the universe. An incredible 95 percent is yet to be discovered!

MIRRORS ON THE MOON

When astronauts visited the moon in the early 1970s, they placed small mirrors on its surface. Scientists on Earth fired laser beams at these mirrors. They used telescopes to time how long the laser beams took to bounce back to Earth. From this answer, they measured the distance from Earth to the moon. It is nearly 250,000 miles (400,000 km).

Light-Years

Space is so big, we need special units to measure it. Distances in space are measured in light-years. A light-year is the distance a beam of light travels in one year. One light-year is about 6 trillion miles (9.5 trillion km). It would take a jet more than a million years to fly that far!

HANDS ON

How Long Is Your Street?

WHAT YOU NEED

- A piece of ribbon
- Scissors
- A bicycle
- A friend to help you
- An adult to walk with you
- A sharp pencil
- A piece of chalk
- A ruler
- A pen and piece of paper

WHAT YOU DO

1. Cut a small length of ribbon using the scissors. Ask an adult to help. Tie the ribbon to the outside of the bicycle tire where you can see it.

2. Turn the bicycle wheel so the ribbon is at the bottom, on the ground. Using the chalk, make a mark on the ground next to the ribbon.

3. Slowly push the bicycle along so the wheel turns around exactly once. The ribbon should move back to the bottom again. With your chalk, make a second mark on the ground, next to the ribbon.

4. Using the ruler, measure the distance between the two chalk marks. This distance is the same as the distance around the edge of your tire, or its circumference. Write down this figure.

5. Take your bicycle to one end of your street. Get an adult to go with you. Turn the tire so the ribbon or tape is at the bottom.

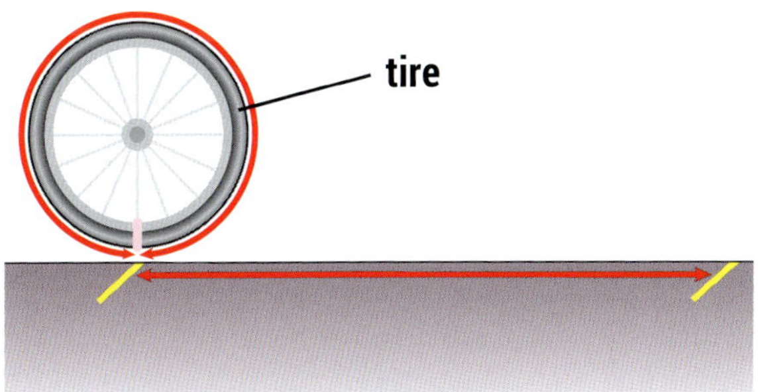

Chalk mark on the street

Ribbon around the tire

Distance between the two chalk marks = circumference of the tire

6. Wheel the bicycle slowly along from one end of the street to the other. Count how many times the ribbon hits the pavement. That is the number of times the wheel has turned around.

7. Multiply the number of times the wheel turned by the circumference of your tire. For example, say your tire's circumference is 25 inches (64 cm) and the wheel has turned around 50 times. The length of your street is:

25 inches x 50

= 1,250 inches (or 104 feet)

or:

64 centimeters x 50

= 3,200 centimeters (or 32 meters)

Glossary

caliper A device for measuring the distance across (width of) an object.

centimeter A small distance equal to one meter divided by 100.

cubit In ancient times, the distance from the tip of a person's middle finger to their elbow.

distance A measurement of the space between two points. Length measures distance across the ground. Height measures distance from top to bottom.

divider A tool for measuring distances on a map.

foot A distance equal to 12 inches. A foot was originally about the length of an adult's foot.

gauge A device for measuring small widths (distances across things).

inch One-twelfth of a foot. An inch was originally the width of an adult's thumb.

kilometer A metric measurement equal to 1,000 meters.

laser beam A very strong and straight beam of light.

light-year The distance light travels in one year, roughly 6 trillion miles (9.5 trillion kilometers).

meter A metric measurement equal to about 3.3 feet.

metric A set of measurements based on the meter.

microscope A scientific instrument for magnifying very tiny things.

millimeter A very small distance equal to 1 meter divided by 1,000 (or 1 centimeter divided by 10).

mile A distance equal to 5,280 feet, or 1,760 yards (1.6 kilometers).

nanometer An extremely tiny distance; one-billionth of a meter.

navigation A way of finding your position on Earth, at sea, or in space.

ruler A straight measuring tool.

satellite An uncrewed spacecraft that can measure things from space.

sextant A device used for navigating at sea. It measures the position of the sun in the sky.

theodolite A device that people use for measuring distances and angles.

yard A distance equal to 3 feet (90 centimeters).

Find Out More

BOOKS

Amstutz, Lisa J.
Rulers and Tape Measures.
Capstone Publishing, 2020.

Murray, Julie.
Measure It! Length.
Abdo Kids Junior, 2019.

Rustad, Martha E. H.
Measuring Length.
Capstone Publishing, 2019.

Scheff, Matt.
Amazing Human Feats of Distance.
Capstone Publishing, 2019.

WEBSITES

www.distance.to
This online calculator figures out the distance between any locations.

www.spacecentre.nz/resources/learn/universe/distances.html
Find out about distances in space.

www.mathsisfun.com/measure/estimate-distance.html
This website shows how to estimate how far away an object is.

Index

ANSWERS

Page 8: 5 feet 9 inches = 69 inches; 18 feet = 18 x 12 = 216 inches; 120 yards = 120 x 3 = 360 feet. **Page 11:** 20.3 cm or 203 mm. Page 13: 6.4 km; 10 cm; 9.6 miles.